Also available in this series from Quadrille:

MINDFULNESS
MINDFULNESS II
QUIET
FRIENDSHIP
LOVE
CONFIDENCE
TIDINESS
HAPPINESS
MOTHERHOOD
LUCK
US
SEX
CHRISTMAS
SISTERHOOD
SELF-CARE
KINDNESS
BRIDESMAIDS
PRIDE

the little book of
GRATITUDE

Hardie Grant

QUADRILLE

Gratitude

Definition:
noun

The quality of being thankful; readiness to show appreciation for and to return kindness.

"Cultivate the habit of being grateful for every good thing that comes to you, and to give thanks continuously. And because all things have contributed to your advancement, you should include all things in your gratitude."

RALPH WALDO EMERSON

'Thank you' around the world

Arabic – shukran

Bulgarian – blagodaria

Czech – děkuji

Danish – tak

Estonian – tänan

French – merci

German – danke

Hindi – dhanyavād / shukriya

Italian – grazie

Japanese – arigatô

Kurdish – spas dikim

Lithuanian – ačiū

Malay – terima kasih

Norwegian – takk

Polish – dziękuję

Romanian – mulțumesc

Spanish – gracias

Turkish – teşekkür ederim

Uzbek – rahmat

Welsh – diolch

Yiddish – a dank

Zulu – ngiyabonga

Gracious

Real

Appreciated

Trusting

Instinctive

Tender

Useful

Delightful

Expressive

Gratitude's root word derives from the Latin *gratus*, meaning: pleasing, welcome, agreeable.

The root gratus also sprouts the words: grace, gratuity and gratis.

Gratitude has an entirely positive etymology and is associated with helpful actions and feelings.

" If the only prayer you ever say in your entire life is thank you, it will be enough."

MEISTER ECKHART

" Do not spoil what you have by desiring what you have not; remember that what you now have was once among the things you only hoped for."

EPICURUS

The word gratitude is etymologically related to the word *gratis* – meaning free. So, remembering to be grateful does not mean to be constantly buying people thank-you gifts. Gratitude is free and can be conveyed without financial outlay: a smile, a word, eye contact will suffice.

Gratitude is:

- an emotion

- a motivator

- a habit

- a moral virtue

- a firewall against negative emotions

- sometimes hard

- always worth striving for

Gratitude walks hand in hand
with humility. Gratitude allows
us to understand that we would
not be who we are without the
help, support and love of others.

Gratitude is the act of acknowledging the goodness in your life. More often than not, the source of the goodness comes, at least partially, from outside of yourself. It is within this 'gap' that thankfulness finds a home and helps us to appreciate how much we rely on others for our own happiness.

Being grateful allows us to look at the world and see benevolence, not forces of hostility and fear.

" Thinking is thanking."

MARTIN HEIDEGGER

Consider thankfulness as a glass of champagne. When the glass of your heart is overflowing with joy, the bubbles of gratitude spill out with abandon.

Gratitude is a tool to help you see what's there instead of what isn't.

Have a grateful heart and it will soon
fill with such joy that you have no
choice but to share it with others.

"Some people are grumbling because roses have thorns; I am thankful that thorns have roses."

ALPHONSE KARR

Consider gratitude as a magic weapon. As Mary Shelley the Romantic writer articulated, we all have the power to inspire feelings of pleasure or pain. Use gratitude as the good fairy would – bestow thankfulness where you can, and with liberality.

" *It is a strange feeling for a girl when first she finds the power put into her hand of influencing the destiny of another to happiness or misery. She is like a magician holding for the first time a fairy wand, not having yet had experience of its potency.* "

MARY SHELLEY

Gratitude can only walk upright when holding the hand of sincerity.

Imagine a life without gratitude. No love would ever be strong enough, no possessions good enough, no house big enough, no salary large enough, no friendship special enough.

Gratitude is a gentle emotion; it does not laugh and shriek like passion but provides a gentle thrum of joy.

Why gratitude is important

We all begin our lives thanks to forces entirely beyond ourselves. Whether our conception is viewed as being in the hands of God, or the gods, or simply the randomness of that egg and that sperm, our very existence is outside of our control. To acknowledge this extraordinary gift of life requires a form of gratitude that is metaphysical in its reach. It is thought that the cosmic destiny of our being provokes instinctive gratitude and as such, gratitude is fundamental to the human condition.

Robert A. Emmons, PhD., is one of the world's leading scientific experts on gratitude. He is a professor of psychology at the University of California, Davis, and the founding editor-in-chief of *The Journal of Positive Psychology*. His research has revealed that people who regularly practise gratitude have vastly improved physical, psychological and social wellbeing.

Physical wellbeing

- Stronger immune systems
- Less bothered by aches and pains
- Lower blood pressure
- Exercise more and take better care of their health
- Sleep longer and feel more refreshed upon waking

Psychological wellbeing

- Higher levels of positive emotions
- More alert, alive and awake
- More joy and pleasure
- More optimism and happiness

Social wellbeing

- More helpful, generous and compassionate

- More forgiving

- More outgoing

- Less loneliness

Great news from neuroscience – when we express gratitude as well as when we receive it, dopamine and serotonin (the happy hormones) are released.

Professor Robert A. Emmons,
the gratitude expert, famously
states that gratitude is the ultimate
performance-enhancing substance.

From childhood to old age, a wide array of psychological, physical and relational benefits are associated with gratitude. Gratitude has been shown to contribute not only to an increase in happiness, health and other desirable life outcomes but also to a decrease in negative affect and problematic functioning.

5 benefits of practising gratitude:

1. Reduced stress
2. Improved sleep
3. Reduced negative emotions
4. Increased physical health
5. Improved relationships

Feeling hopeless, resentful and angry? You have a choice to continue along the emotional road of more pain, more resentment and more anger, or to choose to be grateful for those parts of your mind that are still intact.

Choosing gratitude during a time of suffering offers a pathway out of the pain.

Embrace the virtuous circle of happiness and gratitude. Being grateful leads to happiness and the state of happiness encourages more exuberant gratitude. The gratitude / happiness circle exists in an endless loop.

In social psychology, gratitude is known as a 'prosocial' state and trait – the sort of behaviour that benefits others or society as a whole.

It is understood by psychologists that gratitude helps to motivate people to behave in ways that reciprocate the assistance they receive from others.

Or in simple terms: I thank – you thank; I share – you share; I co-operate – you co-operate.

Exhibiting gratitude is thought by social psychologists to help increase the giver's sense of social worth. By expressing appreciation to the neighbour who brings in your bin, you are in turn increasing your neighbour's sense of social worth. By saying thank you, you are making them feel a useful part of the community.

There is nothing worse than when you are feeling down to be told to 'keep your chin up'. However, if you routinely practise gratitude you will find yourself able to explore its relevance during periods where there seems little to be grateful for.

Utilizing gratitude will help you reframe a negative event as one with potential positive possibilities.

How to incorporate gratitude into your daily life

Be mindful of your interactions with those who serve you. Make a conscious decision never to use your phone, maintain eye contact and always sincerely thank those who help ease your day.

Improve your sleep

Write a positive thought down before bed. Not only will this help you to doze off, but it will send you to sleep with a positive mindset.

Improve your relationships

Practise gratitude within your relationships. Gratitude helps people to foster empathy and compassion and, in turn, to open up and strengthen emotional connections.

Gratitude is about more than good manners. The act of gratitude is like a sticky glue that bonds society closer together. In offering meaningful thanks you form a trusting connection with the recipient and create circuits of pleasure and reward. Communal bonds are strengthened and both you and the person you thanked experience a rush of positive emotion.

Make a gratitude vow

Use a significant date to make a solemn vow to proceed through the year with gratitude. Make a note of your vow, keep it somewhere safe and reread annually.

Example of a gratitude vow

I promise from this day forward to be thankful for the many blessings that have unfolded on my life's path.

I promise to be grateful too for the stones of hardship that can trip me up; they will make my footfalls firmer.

I will show my gratitude, with love and appreciation, to those I meet through life's journey.

> *"The thankful receiver bears
> a plentiful harvest."*

WILLIAM BLAKE

Like most emotions worth cultivating, feelings of gratitude can be attained by simply tuning in.

As mindfulness has taught us, the act of properly tuning in to situations can alert us to positive emotional responses, meaning that when you thank others, they will recognize that you are truly grateful rather than speaking 'thanks' out of habit. And you too will experience genuine gratitude.

Don't wait for the big display of love, or work appreciation, to express gratitude. Try to be equally grateful for the small everyday aspects of life.

Nothing is too small to be grateful for.

Cheers! Thanks! Ta!

Terms of thankfulness trip off tongues but sometimes do not carry their intended meaning – the speaker doesn't look up, is already walking away, is busy with their phone. No matter how many times a day you utter small words of thanks, attempt to couple the speaking with the actions of eye contact and smiling. Suddenly the small words have bigger meanings.

A moaning mouth speaks
of an ungrateful heart.

Conjure time in ways that allow your future self to be grateful to your past self.

When embarking on a course of action that is going to be physically and mentally gruelling, write yourself an encouraging letter. 'I am taking this route (going back to college / working two jobs / leaving a toxic relationship) so that, in one / five / 10 years' time, I will look back from the future and be grateful for the sacrifices I made.' Reread the letter when you feel your present self lose sight of your future.

"Gratitude is not only the greatest of virtues, but the parent of all the others."

CICERO

What are you grateful for?

The early shift. The dishwasher. The wet laundry. The school run. The mad dash to the shop. The late shift. When life seems nothing more than a battering of mundane, thankless tasks, try to make time in your daily routine to reframe these pinch points into moments of gratitude. I'm grateful for my full life of work, family and all the chaos it brings.

Embrace the urgency of gratitude.

If now is not the time to be grateful
– when will be?

There is no need to limit grace to mealtime; offer up thoughts of thankfulness before: walks in the countryside, family gatherings, visits to the theatre; before any activity that enlivens life.

Form grateful motions

As with all good characteristics, gratitude can be learned first by forming good habits. If you struggle to be spontaneously grateful, simply go through the motions.

Look people in the eye when you thank them, send thank-you notes, smile when something is handed to you.

Once outer displays of gratitude are mastered, inner feelings of gratitude will grow.

" Take full account of what Excellencies you possess, and in gratitude remember how you would hanker after them, if you had them not."

MARCUS AURELIUS

Create a gratitude jar

If one of those huge pickling jars is too daunting, go for a small, empty jam jar. Leave a notebook handy beside it and whenever you are struck by a wave of gratitude for something or someone in your life, jot it down. Fold and place it into the jar and watch it fill with whispers of gratitude.

When feeling low, pull out a gratitude memory and remind yourself of reasons to be grateful.

" There is much greatness of mind in acknowledging a good turn, as in doing it."

SENECA

A dog racing across an empty beach, a child in fancy dress, a flower at peak bloom. Become a 'grateful gazer.' Practise the art of pausing and drinking in the moment.

- Stop.

- Gaze.

- Be grateful.

Create visual reminders to be grateful every day

Invest in luminous Post-it notes and write gratitude prompts:

- On the mirror: I am grateful for my confidence

- On the fridge: thank you for the bounty of good food

- On the back of the door: I feel gratitude for the pure possibilities of the day

Gratitude exists in multiple planes of time. Cultivating all three thankfulness time zones will help maintain a positive and optimistic mindset.

The past: recalling positive memories from your childhood.

The present: actively being thankful for the opportunities given.

The future: approaching future challenges with a hopeful viewpoint.

3 free ways of expressing gratitude

1. Can't find the writing paper? Phone has run out of data? Visit your gratitude recipient, knock on their door and tell them simply why you wish to thank them. You needn't write a speech, but your words will be heartfelt and appreciated.

2. Smile your thanks to everyone who assists you.

3. Ask to speak to the manager of the cinema, café or clothes store and express gratitude for the brilliant service you have received.

There is nothing insipid and meek about deciding to be grateful for small pleasures. It is these small aspects that make up the lion's share of life. Whether a cup of tea made by a friend, a funny message from a colleague or a ray of sunlight on a rainy day, dwell for a moment on the pleasure engendered.

Deploy thanks to foster positivity

- Use thanks to accept compliments graciously.

- Use thanks to diffuse lateness – thank you so much for waiting.

- Use thanks to accept criticism – thank you for your comments, let me consider them carefully.

Grateful moments

To be ungrateful is a form of refusal to appreciate what we have. As challenging as life may feel at times, there are always aspects of it that ought to prompt gratitude. Find the small rays of light in dark times and cherish them: the cat purring, a hot chocolate laden with marshmallows, the friendly wave from a neighbour. Consider each carefully and spend a moment being grateful that they are part of your life and that they bring you momentary joy.

Make a note in your journal

This week I am grateful for:

- a thing that made me smile...
- a friend that made me laugh...
- a meal that tasted great...
- a place I felt comfortable...
- a beautiful view I enjoyed...

Make a note in your journal

This year I am grateful for:

- a work achievement...

- a place I've visited...

- a new experience (good or bad)...

- a thing I've learned...

- an event that has made me
feel stronger...

Make a note in your journal

I am grateful for:

- my family because...

- my job because...

- where I live because...

- my community because...

- my body because...

"I would maintain that thanks are the highest form of thought; and that gratitude is happiness doubled by wonder."

G. K. CHESTERTON

"When you are not happy with your life, always think that someone is happy simply because you exist."

FRIEDRICH SCHILLER

Bookend your day with gratitude

Begin each morning by asking:

- Today I am grateful I am going to...

End each day by concluding:

- Today I am grateful for...

Top tip

When investing in a gratitude journal buy the smallest one you can find. That way when the novelty has worn off you're not faced with thick, empty pages guilting you. Keep it short and sweet and buy another when your teeny journal is filled with bite-sized thankful thoughts.

Create a gratitude thread

Every evening log one thing
you are grateful for, either in:

- a journal

- on your phone

- on the wall of your kitchen like
  a child's height chart

- as a screen saver on your laptop

- on Post-it notes around your
  bathroom mirror

Watch the list grow as long or as wide
as your gratitude allows.

Even AI understands the importance of gratitude. Most home AI systems have an inbuilt gratitude feature. Try asking for 'gratitude affirmations', or use the device to begin a 'gratitude log', or accept a 'gratitude challenge'.

Some days it's impossible to feel gratitude for huge concepts such as: the universe, life and love. Rather than thinking in vast terms, cut time down to smaller chunks.

What am I grateful for this week?

Or if this is still too much, ask yourself, 'What am I grateful for this very second?' Take note and experience gratitude in that very immediate moment of time.

2-for-1

So, something upsetting has happened. You are feeling tearful and sad, or furious and vengeful. At this exact moment, remember the 2-for-1 trick: for every bad thing that happens, think immediately of two things to be grateful for.

Exhibiting gratitude in moments of high stress or deep sadness can help ameliorate the pain.

"He who neglects the present moment, throws away all he has."

FRIEDRICH SCHILLER

Gratitude is not limited to sunshine on a rainy day, but extends to clouds and thunder. It is not only the positive events and people we ought to be grateful for, but also the negative events and personalities who stretch our limits and teach us we can survive even in stormy conditions.

List any adversity you've experienced that has since strengthened you and brought unexpected gifts.

List the negative people in your life and consider if your interaction with them has taught you any positive or practical lessons.

List your negative emotions and consider whether you have been able to harness them for good.

Read and contemplate your lists. Ask yourself if you should feel gratitude towards the clouds and thunder that inevitably strengthen and add flair to your character.

The benefits of a good night's sleep are manifold and can be encouraged by grateful thoughts washing through your brain before bed.

Much like the ritual of praying before bed, the ritual of keeping a gratitude journal or chanting the things that you are grateful for can help to flood your mind with happy thoughts that promote a sense of peace and rest. Keeping pre-sleep thoughts upbeat averts the fretfulness and worry that interrupts sleep.

*"Above All Things, O God,
Grant Me a Grateful Heart."*

ancient prayer

Mary Oliver, who won the Pulitzer Prize for Poetry in 1984, wrote a glorious poem entitled 'Gratitude'. Within the poem she asks questions and answers them with divine observations of the natural world.

Her questions can be used as gratitude prompts:

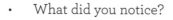

- What did you notice?
- What did you hear?
- When did you admire?
- What astonished you?
- What was most tender?
- What was most wonderful?

Think back to who you were ten years ago, five, two, one, last month, yesterday. You have changed in ways that are astonishing. It is therefore imperative to be grateful for what you currently have, because what needed to be cherished yesterday may well have disappeared today.

Consider gratitude as a muscle: the more you use it, the stronger it grows.

"Feeling gratitude and not expressing it is like wrapping a present and not giving it."

WILLIAM ARTHUR WARD

Never underestimate how much impact on a person's emotional wellbeing an act of gratitude might make. What may be a small effort to you – a hastily written note, a boxed cupcake on their desk, a bunch of wild flowers, for instance – can really light up someone else's day.

The easiest way of showing gratitude is returning that for which you are grateful.

Therefore, return kindness with kindness, charm with charm, patience with patience and watch your gratitude multiply among others.

"Appreciation is a wonderful thing. It makes what is excellent in others belong to us as well."

VOLTAIRE

As a general rule of gratitude – always tip.

Remember, tipping means a lot more to the person being tipped than to you.

Like all attitudes worth nurturing in children, gratitude is better 'caught' than 'taught'.

When to thank someone for:

- a coffee – immediately
- a gift – within a few days
- dinner – within a week
- a wedding present – within a few months of the wedding
- support during a tricky period – when you are ready

"Practise truth, contentment and kindness, this is the most excellent way of life."

Guru Granth Sahib

How to write the perfect thank-you letter

- Make sure you spell their name correctly.

- Get straight to the point. 'Many thanks indeed for...'

- Explain why the act of kindness meant so much to you.
'I was particularly touched to receive this because...'

- Be specific and illuminate how you plan to use the gift. 'It's great timing because I shall be...'

- Keep the giver at the centre of your letter. 'How thoughtful you were to think of such a gift…'

- If appropriate include some other news about yourself and express hope that all is well with them.

- Repeat your thanks briefly and sign off with a warm valediction: best wishes, all the best, yours truly, warm regards.

With gift-giving or acts of kindness, one ought not expect, let alone insist, on being thanked.

"Gratitude is the delightful emotion of love to him who has conferred a kindness on us, the very feeling of which is itself no small part of the benefit conferred."

THOMAS BROWN

5 creative ways of expressing gratitude

1. Turn a photograph into a card and post to a friend with a nice message.

2. No matter how hopeless at singing you may be, record a short burst of 'Thank You for Being a Friend', by Andrew Gold, and send to your friend with love.

3. Customize a pot plant with a ribbon and a gratitude message and leave on your recipient's doorstep.

4. Go old-school and create a photo book of great times spent with the person you wish to thank.

5. Invite friends for dinner and begin the feasting with a special toast to your friend. Raise your glasses in a spirit of gratitude.

Gratitude need not be limited to others, or oneself or the universe. Inanimate objects also deserve our thanks. Precious pieces such as the vast wok that can cook meals for 12 or grandma's best-beloved silver thimble have a potency that deserves to be treasured. Once those special objects have been identified, work out how best you can show them gratitude...

Does the wok need a new handle, can the thimble be polished? Tend to the objects, thank them for their service to you and in doing so you will help ensure they continue to play a vibrant role within your life.

"Gratitude is a duty which ought to be paid, but which none have a right to expect."

JEAN-JACQUES ROUSSEAU

There ought to be no duty within gratitude. We are lucky not to live in an age where we are automatically expected to show gratitude to our 'betters'. Gratitude is hollow if it is simply done by rote.

There is no need to force yourself to be intellectually grateful for something that is causing you emotional pain. If you feel rotten, feel rotten – it's okay to not feel okay. Save gratitude for something else on another day.

"I was complaining that I had no shoes till I met a man who had no feet."

CONFUCIUS

Gratitude can taste bittersweet. It is often experienced when we witness the pain of others. Our friend has suffered a bereavement, our colleague has lost their job, another's child is ill. It is through the suffering of others that we experience gratitude for our own blessings.

Thank yourself

Thanking yourself is just as important as thanking other people.

Gratitude is not limited to other people and how they help you; it should also be expressed inwardly to yourself on a regular basis.

Consider how much happier you would be if, instead of the constant tirade against yourself: 'I must lose weight', 'I must exercise more', 'I must get a promotion', you spoke to yourself in grateful terms: 'thank you for that delicious dinner last night', 'thank you for that short walk yesterday', 'thank you for persevering'.

Set up a self-appreciation society
– the rules and regulations

- This is a very exclusive society with a membership of one.

- It meets on a daily basis.

- Its slogan is 'Thank you for being you'.

- Its code of ethics dictates that the member must speak gratefully to themselves.

- Members are encouraged to record on a daily basis why they are thankful to themselves.

Write letters of thanks to your younger self:

'Dear me, thank you for your hard work at school that has now enabled me to...'

'Dear me, thank you for your strength in saying no to that time that did not work for me...'

'Dear me, thank you for your certainty in deciding to...'

3 ways to express gratitude to yourself

1. Track the gratitude. From the smallest wave from a passerby to a formal letter of thanks, record how people are grateful to you.

2. Set yourself a self-gratitude challenge to praise yourself at least once a day.

3. Thank yourself every evening. After cleaning your teeth at night, look at yourself in the mirror and say: 'Thank you for what you have achieved / enjoyed today.'

Remember the old adage: what you appreciate, appreciates.

Appoint yourself to the position of 'Gratitude Ambassador'. This position needn't be made public; there is no need to announce it to family or colleagues. The role of Gratitude Ambassador is simply to practise gratitude within the home and workplace. It is believed that when family and colleagues witness the Ambassador's attitude of gratitude, they too will adopt thankfulness as part of their daily conversation.

Visualize your body as an external object that transports you, allows you to feel pleasure and keeps your mind alive. By thinking of your body as a separate entity you will be better able to see it as an individual creature that requires gratitude.

Consider your feet and how they have carried you today, how they have safely managed your daily 10,000 steps. How can gratitude be shown to your feet? A footbath, a pedicure, a lovely new pair of shoes.

Consider your hands and how they have made food for you today, how they have typed your thoughts, how they have tended to those you love. How can gratitude be shown to hands? A manicure, a French polish, thick luxurious hand-cream, a delicate henna tattoo, a beautiful new ring.

Consider your stomach and how it has processed the food you need for energy, how it has given you the strength to live well today. How can gratitude be shown to the stomach? Make food from scratch with fresh, tasty ingredients.

Night-time ritual

Lie in a warm, comfortable bed with your hands by your sides.

Close your eyes.

Visualize your body from above and contemplate the good service it has done you that day. Ponder the walks it has taken, the tasks it has completed, the exertions it has experienced.

Begin at the feet and thank each body part individually.

- Thank you feet for taking me where I wanted to go today.

- Thank you legs for carrying me on today's journey.

- Thank you gut for processing the energy I need for life today.

- Thank you heart for beating.

- Thank you arms for embracing those I love.

- Thank you eyes for seeing the beauty around me.

By the time you reach your eyes, your body may have entered a deep state of gratitude and sleep will approach gently.

A grateful heart is a magnet
for miracles.

" *I awoke this morning with devout thanksgiving for my friends, the old and the new.* **"**

RALPH WALDO EMERSON

Gratitude is the heart's memory.

"Gratitude is the best attitude. There is not a more pleasing exercise of the mind than gratitude. It is accompanied with such an inward satisfaction that the duty is sufficiently rewarded by the performance."

JOSEPH ADDISON

" I can no other answer make but thanks, and thanks, and ever thanks..."

WILLIAM SHAKESPEARE
Twelfth Night

" I feel a very unusual sensation – if it is not indigestion, I think it must be gratitude."

BENJAMIN DISRAELI

Express your gratitude with small acts of kindness.

" *I remember, when I was a child and wrote poems in little clasped books, I used to kiss the books and put them away tenderly because I had been happy near them, and take them out by turns when I was going from home, to cheer them by the change of air and the pleasure of the new place. This, not for the sake of the verses written in them, and not for the sake of writing more verses in them, but from pure gratitude.* "

ELIZABETH BARRETT BROWNING

It is arduous to achieve, but be grateful for the darkness that gives light its shine. As the Romantic poet Robert Browning wrote:

" You never know what life means till you die; even throughout life, tis death that makes life live."

ROBERT BROWNING

"Reflect upon your present blessings of which every man has many – not on your past misfortunes, of which all men have some."

CHARLES DICKENS

John Kralik was struggling with setbacks in his personal and work life when he decided to begin a gratitude journal. He set himself the task of writing a handwritten thank you note every day for the next year. His 365 thank-you letters formed the basis of his book *A Simple Act of Gratitude: How Learning to Say Thank You Changed My Life*. He found that acknowledging how his life is bound in with others and expressing gratitude caused blessings to come his way.

"We walk on starry fields of white
And do not see the daisies;
For blessings common in our sight
We rarely offer praises.
We sigh for some supreme delight
To crown our lives with splendour,
And quite ignore our daily store
Of pleasures sweet and tender."

ELLA WHEELER WILCOX
'Thanksgiving'

"I didn't expect to recover from my second operation but since I did, I consider that I'm living on borrowed time. Every day that dawns is a gift to me and I take it in that way. I accept it gratefully without looking beyond it. I completely forget my physical suffering and all the unpleasantness of my present condition and I think only of the joy of seeing the sun rise once more and of being able to work a little bit, even under difficult conditions."

HENRI MATISSE

After an operation prevented him from painting again, he turned to cut-outs and collages and enjoyed a second burst of creativity.

"Courtesies of a small and trivial character are the ones which strike deepest in the grateful and appreciating heart."

HENRY CLAY

Gratitude is not an empty vessel
but a vehicle intent on action.

"*It is better to light one small candle of gratitude than to curse the darkness.*"

CONFUCIUS

The winds of gratitude are always blowing; you merely have to raise the sail.

"Thankfulness is the beginning of gratitude. Gratitude is the completion of thankfulness. Thankfulness may consist merely of words. Gratitude is shown in acts."

HENRI FREDERIC AMIEL

" When upon life's billows you are tempest tossed,
When you are discouraged, thinking all is lost,
Count your many blessings name them one by one,
And it will surprise you what the Lord hath done."

JOHNSON OATMAN JR

Gratitude is a frame of mind that accepts that enough is enough and that more is not always better.

> *"Life is not having and getting but being and becoming."*

MATTHEW ARNOLD

" What bonds of gratitude I feel
No language can declare;
Beneath the oppressive weight I reel,
'Tis more than I can bear:
When shall I that blessing prove,
To return thee love for love?"

WILLIAM COWPER
'Gratitude and Love to God'

"Wake at dawn with a winged heart and give thanks for another day of loving."

KHALIL GIBRAN

Being grateful does not mean accepting less than you are worth, but it does mean being thankful for what you have before striving for more.

"Nothing is more honourable than a grateful heart."

SENECA

*"I thank thee, friend, for the
beautiful thought
That in words well chosen thou
gavest to me,
Deep in the life of my soul it
has wrought
With its own rare essence to ever
imbue me,
To gleam like a star over devious ways,
To bloom like a flower on the
drearest days
Better such gift from thee to me
Than gold of the hills or pearls of
the sea.*

For the lustre of jewels and gold
may depart,
And they have in them no life of
the giver,
But this gracious gift from thy heart
to my heart
Shall witness to me of thy love forever;
Yea, it shall always abide with me
As a part of my immortality;
For a beautiful thought is a
thing divine,
So I thank thee, oh, friend, for this
gift of thine."

LUCY MAUD MONTGOMERY
'Gratitude'

"I thank you, kind and best beloved friend,
With the same thanks one murmurs to a sister,
When, for some gentle favour, he hath kissed her,
Less for the gifts than for the love you send,
Less for the flowers, than what the flowers convey;
If I, indeed, divine their meaning truly,
And not unto myself ascribe, unduly,
Things which you neither meant nor wished to say,
Oh! tell me, is the hope then all misplaced?

*And am I flattered by my own
affection?
But in your beauteous gift, methought I
traced
Something above a short-lived
predilection,
And which, for that I know no dearer
name,
I designate as love, without love's
flame.*"

HENRY TIMROD
'Thank You'

"Rest and be thankful."

WILLIAM WORDSWORTH

A spirit of gratitude indicates
a heart attuned to all that is
good in the universe.

"What a joy it is to feel the soft, springy earth under my feet once more, to follow grassy roads that lead to ferny brooks where I can bathe my fingers in a cataract of rippling notes, or to clamber over a stone wall into green fields that tumble and roll and climb in riotous gladness!"

HELEN KELLER

"As God loves a cheerful giver, so he also loves a cheerful taker. Who takes hold of his gifts with a glad heart."

JOHN DONNE

Gratitude is saying thank you even if no one hears, it is writing a letter that no one may read, it is whispering a prayer of thanks to the empty universe. The thankfulness of your heart is reward enough.

"In everyone's life, at some time, our inner fire goes out. It is then burst into flame by an encounter with another human being. We should all be thankful for those people who rekindle the inner spirit."

ALBERT SCHWEITZER

5 ways to encourage gratitude in the workplace

1. Create a thank-you pinboard.

2. In addition to thanking the member of staff who delivered well, copy in their line manager too.

3. Consider the staff you see every day but have no contact with – the utilities guy, the delivery woman, the security team. Ask their names and thank them for the work they do.

4. Bring in a big box of treats for no reason other than to thank colleagues for their great work.

5. Model grateful behaviour.

Thank the people who never get thanked.

The guy in accounts. The woman who lugs the heavy crate of milk every morning into the coffee shop. The council worker who removes the fly-tipped rubbish. Contemplate those people whose jobs make our lives better and work out how to thank them.

Launch a thank-you circle

Whether at work, at children's activities or in a friendship group, decide to begin every meeting with a thank-you circle. It's very straightforward and simply involves inviting people to share who or what they would like to thank that day. As trust within the circle grows, the gratitude stories will become more meaningful and the bonds within the group will grow.

**3 ways to express gratitude
in the workplace**

1. Get specific. Rather than sending out standard vouchers to all employees, get personal: gardening vouchers for those with green fingers or café vouchers for any caffeine-lovers, for example.

2. Utilize feedback sessions to embed gratitude and appreciation before criticism and goals are discussed.

3. Establish kudos websites or appreciation boards – this all helps to establish an environment that fosters gratitude.

"A grateful mind is a great mind which eventually attracts to itself great things."

PLATO

Itadakimasu

'Itadakimasu' – 'I humbly receive'

There is a charming Japanese custom of saying 'Itadakimasu' – 'I humbly receive' – before a meal. In this moment, there is space to consider and thank all those involved in the preparation of the food, from the fisherman, to the supermarket worker and the chef.

How to perform *Itadakimasu*

- Put your hands together
- Say 'Itadakimasu'
- Bow slightly
- Begin to eat

2 Sanskrit mantras

Dhanya Vad: I feel gratitude

When I am grateful I find grace. By looking for the blessings in my life, I find a space of light in every experience; I open up the path for grace to flow. I make room in the middle of everything for gratitude.

Kritajna Hum: I am gratitude

My true self is always grateful. I am connected with everything else in the universe. I am like an ocean, the deeper I go within the more I connect with the stillness of my true self. Gratitude is the beacon that guides me to the place where meaning, truth and love exist.

Quite the most exquisite demonstration of gratitude is the Loi Krathong floating light festival in Thailand. The origins of the festival are ancient and include giving thanks to the Goddess of Water. The festival, often falling in November, coincides with the end of the rice harvest and is used to thank the Goddess of Water for all the fertility she brings. Bundles of banana leaves are filled with flowers, small offerings of food, incense sticks and a candle, and the krathongs are released across the water in a twinkling display of gratitude.

"Take a close look at today, because yesterday is but a dream and tomorrow is barely a vision."

Sanskrit proverb

"May the gratitude in my heart kiss all the universe."

HAFEZ

The most famous of all festivals of gratitude is the American Thanksgiving tradition, celebrated annually on the fourth Thursday in November. Today, Thanksgiving is a bounteous celebration of family and good fortune inspired by events in 1621.

The votive church of Venice

With over a third of the population of the city killed by the great plague of 1576, the Doge of Venice promised that he would build a church in thankfulness when the plague ended. Doge Alvise I Mocenigo chose Palladio, the finest Renaissance architect, to design the exquisite church of Il Redentore – The Redeemer on a Venetian island.

Every July Venetians celebrate the salvation from the plague with firework displays and decorated gondolas boating out to a church built on gratitude.

The Boll Weevil Monument in Alabama is possibly the world's only monument raised in gratitude to a pest species. In 1915, the boll weevil arrived in Alabama and decimated crops of cotton. While initially a disaster for the farmers, it forced them to diversify and begin to farm other crops such as peanuts. Prosperity came to the town and the monument was raised in 1919 to celebrate success from adversity.

English harvest festivals

Anglo Saxons celebrated 'Lammas' – Loaf-Mass, when the first bread baked from the new harvest was blessed on 1 August. Later, corn dollies were woven and loaves of bread fashioned into sheaves of wheat and a magnificent feast would be enjoyed by the whole community at annual harvest festivals.

Now that food from all over the world can be bought at any time of year, it is hard for us to truly imagine the ecstatic thankfulness that would have been felt at the filling of barns and store cupboards. While harvest festivals are still practised in primary schools and churches, the life-and-death piquancy to the celebrations has been somewhat diminished – and for that we should be grateful.

The end of warfare is always the cause of countrywide thanksgiving celebrations, none more so than the wild parties that spontaneously took place all over Britain on VE Day in 1945. War formally ended in Europe on 7 May and Churchill declared 8 May a public holiday. It was a bittersweet moment with people first heading to churches to pray for those family members they had lost, before enjoying street parties, leaping into fountains or dancing the conga around Trafalgar Square, London.

In thanks for Britain's support for Norway during the Second World War, the Scandinavian kingdom sends a gigantic Norwegian spruce to stand in Trafalgar Square. This gift of gratitude has been the centrepiece of London's Christmas decorations since 1947.

In a gesture of appreciation to the scientist whose understanding of gravity allowed space travel, astronaut Tim Peake took apple seeds from Sir Isaac Newton's famous apple tree to the International Space Station and then, on his return to Earth, planted the saplings in the garden of Newton's home.

During the Covid-19 lockdown of 2020, gratitude to health and key workers was expressed by a Thursday night clapping ritual, across the UK. Neighbours would stand on their doorstep to clap. As the weeks went on the clapping became more boisterous with saucepans and horns being deployed, accompanied by whoops and cheers. It became a ritual that those enduring lockdown appreciated as much as those being thanked.

"Gratitude bestows reverence, allowing us to encounter everyday epiphanies, those transcendent moments of awe that change forever how we experience life and the world."

JOHN MILTON

The deepest sense of gratitude comes to us when we have discovered who we are and our place in the world.

5 Gratitude TED Talks

1. '365 Days of Thank You' Brian Doyle

2. 'Want to be Happy? Be Grateful' David Steindl-Rast

3. 'The Power of Saying Thank You' Laura Trice

4. '365 Grateful Project' Hailey Bartholomew

5. 'Two Words That Can Change Your Life' Tanmeet Sethi

Be more grateful

Gratitude is much more than being thankful; it is a choice and a way of thinking and feeling. It can move us away from negative emotions such as fear and anxiety, and move us towards positivity, understanding, joy and hope.

QUOTES ARE TAKEN FROM

Albert Schweitzer 1875–1965, German humanitarian

Alphonse Karr 1808–1890, French writer

Benjamin Disraeli 1804–1881, Victorian British prime minister

Charles Dickens 1812–1870, English writer of *Oliver Twist*

Confucius 551 BC–479 BC, Ancient Chinese Sage

Cicero 106 BC–43 BC, Roman orator and lawyer

Elizabeth Barrett Browning 1806–1861, Victorian poet

Ella Wheeler Wilcox 1850–1919, American author and poet

Epicurus 341 BC–270 BC, Ancient Greek philosopher

Friedrich Schiller 1759–1805, German playwright and polymath

G. K. Chesterton 1874–1936, English writer

Hafez 1315–1390, Persian poet

Helen Keller 1880–1968, American author and disability rights campaigner

Henri Frederic Amiel 1821–1881, Swiss moral philosopher

Henri Matisse 1869–1954, French artist

Henry Clay 1777–1852, American statesman

Henry Timrod 1828–1867, American poet

Jean-Jacques Rousseau 1712–1778, French philosopher

John Donne 1572–1631, English poet and scholar

John Milton 1608–1674, English poet, author of *Paradise Lost*

Johnson Oatman Jr. 1856–1922, American musical artist

Joseph Addison 1672–1719, English essayist

Khalil Gibran 1883–1931, Lebanese writer

Lucy Maud Montgomery 1874–1942, Canadian author of Anne of Green Gables

Marcus Aurelius 121–180, Roman Emperor and Stoic philosopher

Martin Heidegger 1889–1976, German philosopher

Mary Oliver 1935–2019, American poet

Mary Shelley 1797–1851, English writer and author of *Frankenstein*

Matthew Arnold 1822–1888, English writer and scholar

Meister Eckhart 1260–1328, German theologian

Plato c. 428 BC–c. 348 BC, Ancient Greek philosopher

Ralph Waldo Emerson 1803–1882, American essayist

Robert Browning 1812–1889, English poet

Seneca 4BC–65 AD, Roman Stoic philosopher

Thomas Brown 1778–1820, Scottish philosopher

Voltaire 1694–1778, French philosopher

William Arthur Ward 1921–1994, American writer of maxims

William Blake 1757–1827, English poet

William Cowper 1731–1800, English poet

William Shakespeare 1564–1616, English playwright extraordinaire

William Wordsworth 1770–1850, English Romantic poet

BOOKS AND ARTICLES REFERRED TO

The Gratitude Project: How Cultivating Thankfulness Can Rewire Your Brain for Resilience, Optimism, and the Greater Good, by Jeremy Adam Smith, published by New Harbinger, 2020

Gratitude Works!: A 21-Day Program for Creating Emotional Prosperity, by Robert A. Emmons, published by Jossey-Bass, 2013

The Oxford Dictionary of Quotations, published by OUP, 2004

Thanks!: How Practicing Gratitude Can Make You Happier, by Robert A. Emmons, published by Mariner Books, 2008

A Simple Act of Gratitude: How Learning to Say Thank You Changed My Life, by John Kralik, published by Hachette USA, 2011

The Gratitude Jar: A Simple Guide to Creating Miracles, by Josie Robinson, published by Wise Ink, 2014

'Virtues, Work Satisfactions and Psychological Wellbeing Among Nurses', an article in *The International Journal of Workplace Health Management* by Ronald J. Burke, Eddy S. W. Ng, Lisa Fiksenbaum, ISSN: 1753-8351, 2009

'Gratitude' by R. A. Emmons, J. Froh and R. Rose, in M. W. Gallagher and S. J. Lopez (eds), Positive Psychological Assessment: A Handbook of Models and Measures, pp. 317–332, published by the American Psychological Association, 2019

'A Little Thanks Goes a Long Way: Explaining Why Gratitude Expressions Motivate Prosocial Behavior', an article in *The Journal of Personality and Social Psychology* by Adam Grant and Francesca Gino, 2010

USEFUL WEBSITES

Archive.org

Britannica.com

Dickensletters.com

Forbes.com

Gratefulness.org

Gratitudechallenge.com

Greatergood.berkeley.edu

Happify.com

Positivepsychology.com

Scholar.google.com

Thnks.com

Publishing Director Sarah Lavelle
Editor Stacey Cleworth
Editorial Assistant Sofie Shearman
Words Joanna Gray
Series Designer Emily Lapworth
Junior Designer Alicia House
Head of Production Stephen Lang
Production Controller Sabeena Atchia

Published in 2021 by Quadrille,
an imprint of Hardie Grant
Publishing

Quadrille
52–54 Southwark Street
London SE1 1UN
quadrille.com

Compilation, design, layout and text
© 2021 Quadrille

The publisher has made every
effort to trace the copyright
holders. We apologize in advance
for any unintentional omissions
and would be pleased to insert the
appropriate acknowledgement in
any subsequent edition.

Cataloguing in Publication Data:
a catalogue record for this book is
available from the British Library.

ISBN 978 1 78713 736 3

Printed in China